I0166066

Association Munson

1637-1896. Proceedings of the 2d Munson family reunion,

Held in the city of New Haven, Wednesday, August 19, 1896 - Vol. 2

Association Munson

1637-1896. Proceedings of the 2d Munson family reunion,
Held in the city of New Haven, Wednesday, August 19, 1896 - Vol. 2

ISBN/EAN: 9783337733650

Printed in Europe, USA, Canada, Australia, Japan

Cover: Foto ©ninafisch / pixelio.de

More available books at **www.hansebooks.com**

1637

1887   1896

PROCEEDINGS

OF

THE SECOND

Munson Family Reunion

HELD IN THE

CITY OF NEW HAVEN

WEDNESDAY, AUGUST 19, 1896

————

NEW HAVEN :
THE TUTTLE, MOREHOUSE & TAYLOR PRESS
1896

Chairman.

The Rev. Frederick Munson, - - Brooklyn, N. Y.

Vice-Chairman.

Mr. Rowland B. Lacey, - - - Bridgeport, Conn.

———

1. VOLUNTARY—Piano,
   Prof. Willard L. Munson, Branford, Conn.

2. FAMILY WORSHIP,
   The Rev. A. Monson Griffith, Sabina, Ohio.

3. ADDRESS OF WELCOME, - - - - The Chairman.

4. RESPONSE, - Hon. Gilbert D. Munson, Zanesville, Ohio.

5. SINGING—"O God, beneath Thy guiding hand."

6. HISTORICAL ADDRESS,
   Clarence Munson Bushnell, Esq., Buffalo, N. Y.

7. SECRETARY'S REPORT.

8. SINGING—"My country, 'tis of thee."

9. ANNOUNCEMENTS.

10. BENEDICTION.

EXERCISES.

C. LaRue Munson, Esq., called the meeting to order, and introduced the Rev. Frederick Munson as presiding officer.

On taking the chair, the Rev. Mr. Munson said:

LADIES AND GENTLEMEN, *Brothers and Sisters of the Munson Family:*

I esteem it a great honor to have been chosen by the committee of arrangement to preside at this our second Family Reunion. The honor is all the greater because wholly unexpected and a complete surprise, and will be the more valued if I am able to perform the duties of the position in such a manner as to receive your approval and promote your enjoyment of the occasion.

FAMILY WORSHIP

was conducted by the Rev. Absalom Monson Griffith.

ADDRESS OF WELCOME.

By THE CHAIRMAN.

It is now my privilege to extend to you all, and to each of you, a hearty and sincere welcome. I am happy to be, in this, the voice of those to whom this duty may more especially belong. Indeed it may be difficult, if not impossible, to draw at this time any specific distinction between host and guest. Are we not unitedly, and with one accord, the host, hospitable, bounteous, and free of such as we possess, and giving the true welcome with open hand and open heart? And are we not equally guests, made to feel at home and set at ease by the kindly and gracious reception accorded us? The gentlemen of the committee, who with much labor and pains have made the arrangements for this second reunion of the family, are certainly entitled to be regarded as of the host, and with them the modestly styled coadjutor, the Rev. Myron A. Munson, the family historian and biographer, who, with an amount of toil and perseverance that cannot be measured, has produced a voluminous work which in its line is of unequalled excellence. To be associated with these in constituting the host of this occasion are all those who in any way have given effective aid in bringing about this family reunion and promoting its objects. And yet it may be positively affirmed that no one of these desires to be other than a guest.

Were there now present any of our kindred from beyond the sea, from the fair kingdom whence came our common ancestor to make his home upon these shores, it might be said to them, Welcome to this pleasant land, these broad domains stretching from ocean to ocean and from the lakes to the gulf ; welcome to the grand spectacles presented by its noble rivers, its broad plains, its lofty mountains, and the many wonders of nature in some of their sublimest manifestations ; welcome to this home of liberty under just and equitable laws, and of plenty at most times for the industrious in the various employments and callings that invite exertion and promise rewards ; welcome to the tokens of a civilization, which, as presented in our cities and towns, our varied manufactures, our many forms of business, our social and domestic life, our advance in science and art, our seats of learning, our vast railways and magnificent steamers, is worthy of its origin in the land from which it was transplanted, and is full of promise for the future ; welcome to all that is here presented to cheer the peoples of the nations and to increase the hopes of mankind. The welcome would surely be given with a warmth and cordiality of greeting forever prohibitive of discord and strife.

To you who come from other states, near or remote, of our common country, I may say, Welcome to this State of Connecticut, one of the original thirteen which are represented by the thirteen stripes of alternate white and red upon the old flag, and feeling a sisterly affection for all the states, both old and new, which are radiant in the stars of our glorious banner. A native of this state, and grateful for all that has made it honorable and noteworthy, I may fitly bid you welcome to an acquaintance with its thrifty and intelligent people, its common schools, its varied industries, its academies and colleges, and its institutions for special instruction and professional study. Welcome to the state whose foundations were laid by those of strong faith and high character, such as were Capt. Thomas Munson, his wife Joanna, and those descendants of theirs who were active in influence during the formative period of this old commonwealth.

We bid you welcome also to this beautiful city of New Haven, where our honored ancestor had his home during the greater part of his useful and active life, where, as shown by copious early records of the town cited at large by our pains-taking historian, he was prominent in public affairs, leader of the military forces and frequently in active service for the security of the city against the savage foe, largely trusted as an administrator and friend in social and family interests, and repeatedly through many years was elected to high offices in the town and in the colony by the suffrages of his fellow citizens. Welcome also to the famous university, Old Yale, whose modern and ornate buildings, replacing the plain brick row of former years, stand in gradually increasing numbers upon the campus or quadrangle near this celebrated green, while other edifices of the same great institution may be seen in almost every direction from that classic space of central interest. Welcome to Yale, so far as my enjoyment of its privileges many years ago may give me the right to utter it. The stately buildings invite your observation. Its many departments, each a great institution, indicate the breadth of instruction, mental training and fine culture which it provides. Its libraries and cabinets will awaken a new ambition in any susceptible young mind, and draw forth the desire to drink at such a fountain, whether here or elsewhere. Welcome to any worthy and noble impulse which Yale University can give you.

There have been changes among us since the reunion of nine years ago. In some of our homes and among our near kindred loved ones have passed away. Some who were here on the former occasion, whose voices were then heard, and whose presence and smiles increased the gladness, are with us no more. We drop a tear to their memory. We think of them with the comfort of hope. We bless our Heavenly

Father for what they were with us, and for what, as we trust, they now are in the home above. We feel a deep sympathy with those, our brothers and sisters, whose hearts in these bereavements have been pierced with unutterable sorrows. May divine consolations allay the sharpness of their grief.

There is one more welcome which I would fain give, a welcome to all the influences for good flowing from the life, the character, the usefulness, and the bright example of our ancestor whom we commemorate, who as a young man was one of the pioneers in this city and in organizing its civil and religious institutions, and who in the various experiences of life, whether joyous or afflictive, grew in mental and moral strength, in all manly qualities, and in the esteem and confidence of his contemporaries who continuously called him to high duties for the furtherance of the public welfare. In this present reunion we have an advantage over that of 1887 in an increased knowledge of our ancestor through the publication of the Family Record which so fully portrays him. We stand before that likeness with reverence. We give thanks to God for what he was and for what he was enabled to do. Welcome, then, to the inspiration to a true nobility of living which here comes from the fine record of a genuine life as seen in the course of our common ancestor, Capt. Thomas Munson.

RESPONSE.

By Judge Gilbert D. Munson.

As we listened to those warm words of welcome, two names, I am sure, suggested themselves to all of our minds, connecting the past with the present—Capt. Thomas Munson and Rev. Myron A. Munson. The old pioneer, Capt. Thomas Munson, stands before us, as if in full life. The magic pen of his learned descendant, Rev. Myron A. Munson, has wrought the vision. Conjured by the logic of hard, indisputable facts, Capt. Thomas Munson, that valuable citizen, that efficient soldier, that wise legislator, that upright judge, is in our midst, is here, with his family, to-day, taking part in these festivities. By genealogical lines not to be disputed, he was our ancestor, and this welcome is first of all because of *him;* and next to him, it is because of his biographer, our historian. Therefore, commemorating him whose resplendent character and renown furnish the shining basis of our reunions, and with grateful recognition of him who has traced for each and all of us our right to attend them, and in behalf of all the Family, Mr. President, I return our hearty thanks for the noble welcoming address delivered by you.

This is our second reunion. Nine years ago, was held our first ; and we are to be congratulated upon holding a second. Family pride based upon real merit in ancestors, is a good thing. It establishes an *esprit de corps* not easily broken away from. On that basis, we have just cause, if I may be pardoned in saying it, for proper family pride, and should continue these reunions.

Our ancestor's whole life was a life of merit. His was a grand life, because in common with those of other pioneers, it was actuated by a grand idea, the idea of equality before the law. That idea led to the independence of church and state ; to the Declaration of Independence ; to the Revolutionary War ; to our Civil War ; and will be consummated in the fullness of time, as I verily believe, in courts of arbitration, and in a grand court of international arbitration, when reason shall fight the only battles fought among the children of men, and wars and rumors of wars be heard of to trouble and distress us no more forever, but universal peace prevail.

I say this because sympathy is the direct development of the idea of equality ; and there is to-day greater sympathy throughout our land than was ever known before. This is evidenced by higher social bodies or organizations, intellectual and moral, by means of which we are nearing that ideal state, in which all men, and women too, shall be so absolutely equal before the law, as to be able in fact to pursue each his or her happiness unobstructed.

The time has already arrived when instead of men of war, men of pacific measures are most useful. The time is now here when the whole machinery of civil government may be set in motion, if need be, to right the wrongs of an innocent child, or prevent war with a mighty foreign power, as the case may be. And the time is rapidly approaching when sympathy broad and deep, the development of equality before

2

the law, shall compel the human heart to feel the griefs and joys of the whole sentient universe, and to know no peace while pain and suffering are at hand, imploring relief.

Our Family root is imbedded in an idea producing such results as these. Why, of all the wondrous things born or developed in the interim between 1685 and 1896, sympathy portends most for mankind, because it portends the ideal commonwealth, and, as its consummation, altruistic triumph everywhere.

Now if I am right in this view,—of the development of the idea which actuated our ancestor,—could family tree be deeper set, in more prolific soil? Then I submit we have just cause for proper family pride; and for the reason given, as well as for others equally good, these reunions of the Family should be promoted, fostered, and continued.

I thank you, again, for our cordial welcome.

ORATION.

OUR ANCESTRAL HISTORY.

By Clarence Munson Bushnell, Esq.

WERE the most gifted of our family to stand to-day in the place that the favor of the committee has assigned me, he would find himself poor in words to express the pleasure which I feel in meeting for the first time so many of the descendants of our illustrious ancestor, and my appreciation of the right to share with you the distinction of his name. Perhaps to none of those who have gathered here to do honor to his memory does this meeting mean so much as it does to him who is permitted to address you. Many of you were born within the shadows of the ancestral home, and many more have remained within the boundaries of our native state. You have dwelt among the traditions of the family. In story you have gone forth with Thomas Munson against the Pequots to the banks of the Mystic river. You have seen him raised from the rank of private to that of lieutenant and of captain, and finally you have seen him placed in command of the New Haven county soldiery of the standing army. You have stood guard with him at Saybrook, and accompanied him upon the march to Suckquackheeg. You have discerned his figure in the thickest gloom of King Philip's war. Nightly, for years, as the shades of evening stole over this infant city, you have seen him march forth to set the "watch." You have sat with him upon the bench of the Plantation court and upon the bench of the Court of Appeals. Step by step you have followed his career as soldier, as legislator, as jurist, as citizen. You have had ever before you the records of the confidence reposed in him by his fellow-men and by the officials of the colony. You have stood beneath the elms that sheltered his home; you have walked by his side upon The Green; you have knelt in worship in the church of which he was a member; and at the close of his eventful life you saw him borne to his final rest.

The simple stone that through the centuries succeeding his death has marked his grave, and has told the stranger as he passed it only of his name and span of life, has been to you a silent but constant and solemn reminder of the obligations imposed by his memory.

Not so with those of his descendants whose ancestors in the early generations left the state of Connecticut and made for themselves a home among strangers. Separated from the family and the associations of youth, the recollections of kindred gradually grew fainter and at last died out in their children. Doubtless many of those before me, like myself, have come to-day for the first time to the home of our forefathers. Until now I have chanced to meet only seven persons older than myself who bore the name of Munson. But it detracts nothing from my estimate of the family character that it is based largely upon the life of her from whom are derived my highest conceptions of womanhood.

Until within the last few years, the possession by the average American of even the slightest knowledge of his ancestry was considered almost an offense against our social customs.

A celebrated French scholar and observer who recently visited this country for the purpose of studying our institutions and people says that when an American has nothing to do for a long half day, he sits down and wonders who his grandfather was. If we seek among the beginnings of the Republic for the causes of this apparent lack of hereditary pride, we may find many which imply neither forgetfulness nor disregard of the memory and worth of our fathers. Chief, perhaps, among them is the fact that the records of colonial New England throw so little light upon the lineage of her people, that it is scarcely possible for any one, except by years of patient labor, to trace his descent back through the earlier generations. Were it not for the records of the various towns, meager and imperfect though they be, he who undertakes the task would learn oftentimes only by half-legendary tradition of the existence even of those ancestors whose lives shed brightest lustre on their family name. Perchance he might learn of their birth from the records of the church, and from the humble headstones in the graveyard which surrounds it he might fix the dates of their death, but beyond these he could seldom go. History tells us no more of the lives and sacrifices of many of those of the earlier days whose achievements would have won for them in the old world the proudest titles that royal favor could bestow.

Another cause may be found, but half concealed, beneath the popular interpretation of that phrase in our Declaration of Independence, that "all men are created equal." As an American, proud of the land of my nativity and jealous of her place among the nations of the earth and of her future, I trust that the hour may never come when the sublime truth embodied in these words shall not be recognized as the fundamental principle of our government. But to contend, simply because under our laws all men are accorded equal legal rights and privileges, that all social, moral and intellectual distinctions are to be disregarded, is to pervert the meaning of the declaration and to assail the very foundations of society. Under no form of government are the vicious equal to the virtuous, the ignorant to the enlightened, the anarchist to the patriot. How soon would the republic of America take her place among the dead republics of the past and become a silent tenant of history's page, if she could not, in her hours of need, call to her aid the descendants of the men who laid the foundations of her present power and greatness. If the sacrifices of the fathers in behalf of their country and liberty do not stimulate a loftier patriotism in the hearts of their sons than in the bosoms of strangers, we should do them the justice to speak no more aloud their names, nor claim the benefits of their labors, but by our silence make the confession that we are faithless to the one and unworthy the glory of the other.

Another cause, perhaps as potent as either of those I have named, is that until within a very recent period the energies of the American people have been directed to practical questions of government and to the development of the wonderful resources of our country.

In an address delivered in the city of Buffalo last month, Brander Matthews truly said that "American literature is now but little older than the three score years and ten allotted as the span of a man's natural life." Irving's Sketch-Book and Cooper's Spy did not appear until several years after the beginning of the present century. Previous to this the intellectual development of the country had assumed mainly the theological form, with the exception of oratory, which was born at the epoch of the Revolution. In 1775, one hundred and fifty-five years after the landing of the Pilgrims, there were but thirty-seven newspapers in circulation in the entire country. Unaided, except by the data preserved by analists, by the writings of Ramsey and of Marshall, and by the researches of Grahame, Bancroft, born in 1800, entered the rich field of American history. But until within the last ten or fifteen years, our historical writings have been confined almost exclusively to the leading facts in our national growth; to a backward glance at the state of Europe, the causes of emigration, and the standard of political and social advancement in the colonies. This told only the story, grand as it was, of a people, but left untold or to tradition the individual deeds of valor and of patriotism of all except the few who stood in the full midday light of history. It appealed to the pride of an American as a citizen, but it did not arouse his personal pride as a descendant of the men who won from oppression and wrong the government which for a century past has represented the highest aspirations of humanity. It told of the flight to Leyden and of the landing at Plymouth, of the colonial wars and of the Revolution; but it did not connect him with those events. With increased leisure and the means of education and research, and with the great interest that has been awakened in the study of local history, traditions have been verified, family genealogies have been compiled, and the descendants of the men of New England who early crossed the Hudson, the Mohawk, and the Susquehanna, and later passed beyond the Alleghanies and over the Sierra Nevada, have recently learned for the first time of the true relation that they bore to the mighty struggle of humanity in the sixteenth and seventeenth centuries, which culminated in the republic of America.

At once Colonial and Revolutionary patriotic organizations were formed, historical societies multiplied, priceless records that had remained in manuscript for centuries were printed, local data were collected, arranged and published, suitable monuments were erected to the memory of the heroes and statesmen of the past, and tablets placed upon the spots where the chief events of our history had taken place. With these have come a deeper and more intense spirit of national attachment, of Americanism; a more intelligent appreciation of the labors, the sacrifices, and the triumphs of those who have preceded us, and naturally to many a feeling of hereditary pride. While I would not be understood as favoring the adoption in this country of social grades and distinction similar to those that prevail in the old world, based either upon wealth, the achievements of ancestors, or family name, I would abate in no degree the feelings of honest pride of birth in him who traces his lineage to Pilgrim or to Puritan, to Cavalier or to Revolutionary sire.

I shall not attempt upon this occasion, pleasant as would be the theme, to recount the deeds of the different members of our own family, or to relate the part they have borne in the great events of the past. That task has been performed with so much skill and learning, with such rare discrimination and exhaustive research, by the historian of our family, that no one, for many years at least to come, may venture to walk by his side in that field of inquiry. Great as is our sense of obligation to Myron A. Munson, the full appreciation of his work will come only with succeeding generations, to which, but for his patient toil, the records of our family would doubtless have been lost forever. However much he may owe to those who have preceded him, I believe that the two volumes that bear his name will long be accepted as standards in their department of literature.

Unaware even of my relationship to our honored ancestor until informed by him, and with no means at my command for original research, I can in no particular amplify his work. But as I read again in his pages the history of the earlier days as illustrated by the lives of those whose name we bear, there came to me new interest in the story, a feeling of personal responsibility to the men of prior times, and a truer appreciation of the dignity of American manhood and citizenship. And to-day, although fully mindful of the fact that there is no place in this country where American history is studied with greater zeal, or more clearly understood than at this ancient seat of learning, I ask you to go back with me to the days of Thomas Munson and look for a moment at the influences which guided and governed the men of that period in their work of laying the foundations of this mighty nation. Two centuries separate their labors from ours. We have outlived the prophecy of De Maistre and survived the ordeal which de Tocqueville foresaw and feared; but we have still to contend with the dangers which lurk in an expansion of the Republic in population, domain and wealth, dangers born of peace, not of conflict—of strength, not of weakness—dangers which I believe can be averted or overcome only by keeping alive in the breasts of their descendants the spirit which governed, controlled and dominated their lives.

History furnishes us with no other instance of a nation founded by men of character comparable to that of the men who composed the New England colonies. "God," said William Stoughton, in 1688, "sifted a whole nation

that He might send choice grain into the wilderness."
While it is doubtless true that the Pilgrims "dreamed
not of empire" when they left their place of exile
in Holland and crossed the ocean, yet they brought
with them the spirit of liberty which in a hundred
forms was then hovering over the nations of the old
world. Although they came seeking only freedom
to worship God in their own way, the Pilgrim and
the Puritan brought with them in addition to the free
church the free school; and from these arose, in obedi-
ence to the inexorable logic of Puritanism, the free
state. No words express with half the eloquence, no
subsequent event illustrates with half the force, the devotion and the courage of our Pilgrim Fathers as does the
simple fact that, although returning spring was welcomed
by but half of those who had landed in December, and
only five of these were left in sufficient health to close the
eyes of the dying and bear them to their nameless graves,
yet when the Mayflower returned to England in April
she bore not homeward a single Pilgrim. Is it strange
that principles nurtured by so sublime a faith and de-
fended by such dauntless courage should have survived
the attacks of the savage, triumphed in the war of the
Revolution, and subjected the continent to their sway?

It cannot with fairness be claimed that our government
was founded solely on Puritan teachings. Doctrines and
ideas came from other sources. We must not forget the
grave at Monticello or the tomb at Mount Vernon; and
let us ever remember that the first proclamation in this
country of freedom in religious thought and worship
came not from Protestant New England, but from Catholic Maryland, which declared that "No one in this prov-
ince who believes in Jesus Christ shall be molested in the
free exercise of his or her religion."

But after accrediting to the other forces that have aided
in our growth the full measure even of their claims, to
New England still must be accorded the glory of having
contributed more to the development of our national
character, institutions and government than all the other
agencies combined.

3

The true character of the Puritan has been, perhaps, as often concealed by unmerited praise as by unwarranted detraction. The life of Thomas Munson, as depicted by our historian, presents a faithful portrait of the typical Puritan. As disclosed to us it is invested with neither mystery nor romance. From the day that he first emerges from obscurity at the age of twenty-five until his death at seventy-three, his biography is but the story of unswerving devotion to the colony and to his God. And this is the story of Puritanism. Of what they suffered and endured, harassed by Indians, beset by death in every form, cut off from civilization and beyond the knowledge of their friends and of mankind, we need not speak; their glory springs not from what they endured, but from the fact that they endured it; not from what they suffered, but from what they accomplished; not from the memories which they left behind them, but from those they have handed down to us.

The foremost trait of character that distinguished our ancestors was their profound religious faith, and from this has arisen most of the misapprehension that surrounds their character. Although the Puritans may justly be charged with intolerance, they cannot be accused of inconsistency. They came to this country, not for the purpose of founding a colony in which any one might worship God as he pleased, but for the purpose of securing freedom to worship God in their own way. Religious tolerance was not taught in the fierce school of oppression in which they had been reared. For the purpose of securing freedom of worship, they fled from England to Holland; and that they might preserve among their children the language and traditions of their native land, they came to this country. Their purpose was to found a theocratic state in which the minutest details of their daily life should be regulated by their interpretation of Holy Writ; and although they brought with them the germs of civil as well as of religious liberty, nothing could have been farther from their thoughts than the institution of a government that would condemn to death the judges, jurors and witnesses who participated in the trials for witchcraft, and would command them to take their place on the scaffold on Gallows Hill by the side of their hapless victims—a government that stands proud and imperious among the nations of the earth, yet guards with equal solicitude the religious rights and views of Gentile and of Jew, of Protestant and of Catholic, of Christian and of Infidel. Could they have foreseen the ultimate result of their labors, history would probably contain no mention of the voyage of the Mayflower. While we may not justify their stern religious fanaticism, . their memory pleads for no apology at our hands. By their lives they have made even the name "fanatic" illustrious.

Inseparable from their religious views, and grounded upon them, was their spirit of independence. But this trait of character was to them an inheritance. If we would seek its origin, we must turn our eyes far away from the shores of New England and look much farther back in English history than the establishment of the church at Scrooby Manor or the flight to Holland. More than two centuries before James I. declared at Hampton Court that he would make the Puritans "conform or harry them out of the land," it had challenged the Roman dogma of spiritual supremacy and ushered in the heroic age of England. Slowly and quietly it gathered strength during succeeding reigns, stayed not by persecution or oppression, appalled not by the terrors of the dungeon, the sword or the faggot, until it struggled up to victory on the battle field of Marston Moor and Naseby and ascended with Cromwell the throne of England. It was this same spirit which in 1636 dotted the harbor of Boston with forts in opposition to the schemes of Charles I. to annul the charter of Massachusetts and gave to Beacon Hill its name; that later found expression on the lips of Otis, of Adams and of Patrick Henry; that stood fire at Concord and at Lexington, and is commemorated by the shaft on Bunker Hill; that called Putnam from the plow, Stark from the hills of New

Hampshire, and Greene from his home in Rhode Island; that "smote for liberty" at Trenton, that withstood the sufferings of Valley Forge, that stormed the enemy's works at Stony Point, that sailed the seas with the brave Paul Jones, that won at Monmouth, that received the sword of Cornwallis at Yorktown; and that, at last, as if to rear with its own hands a monument upon which should be forever transfixed the gaze of all mankind, incarnated itself in the life of that matchless figure of the centuries, George Washington.

Closely interwoven with the religion of the Puritans and their ideas of government, was their love of education. According to their theory of life, ignorance was the basis of both popery and despotism. By the side of the church they built the school-house, thus laying the foundation of our system of public schools, in which to-day are taught to sixteen millions of our young not only the English language but the principles of liberty as well. Compulsory education was born in the little colony of Connecticut long before it was even thought of by Frederick of Prussia. In direct opposition to the theory of society which prevailed in the countries of Europe, that the great body of the people should have no part in the government of church or state, and were better kept in ignorance, the New England colonies declared that the state could not endure the results of ignorance in her citizens, and provided the common schools for the common people. Deny if you will to our forefathers all praise save that which rests upon what they did in behalf of education, and you have left them still enough to entitle them to the grateful remembrance of mankind. Light and darkness cannot dwell together. In the common schools of the colonies was fostered the spirit that animated the Revolution and made us free. But it was reserved for a later century to demonstrate the full value of these infant seminaries of liberty. When the supreme test of our institutions came, when the descendant of the Puritan met face to face upon the field of battle the descendant of the Cavalier, and "the hearts of men stood still," it was the love of country taught in our common schools that won.

Permit me here to record my dissent from the assumption which universally prevails and which found expression in Professor Shaler's article in the June number of the North American Review on "Environment and Man in New England," to the effect that slavery was only an accident of soil and climate, and that if the Puritans had settled in Jamestown they would have become its advocates and defenders. I do not believe it. The principles upon which slavery rested were incompatible with the fundamental principles of Puritan belief. Slavery did exist in early New England, but New England arose above it and discarded it, not simply because it was unprofitable, but because it was odious and hateful to the religious faith of her people, condemned by their spirit of independence, and opposed by the teachings of her common schools and colleges. And if the people of New England, throughout all their history, have been distinguished by one characteristic more than by another, it is their willingness to sacrifice material interests to what they believe to be right. Slavery comported with the habits, the training and the more seductive life of the Cavalier, but it could not fasten its roots in the soil of New England, to whose sons, then as now, wealth, ease and position come, if they come at all, as the reward of persistent personal effort. Even if slavery had become one of the fixed institutions of New England, she would have outgrown it and thrown it off, as it was thrown off by England, whose soil, long before our own, became too sacred for the footsteps of the slave.

Religion, liberty and education, these were the forces which dominated the colony founded by the Agreement which bears the name of our honored ancestor; and these were the forces which sustained her sister colonies and which to-day characterize the descendants of New England wherever found. The creation of the political institutions by which liberty is maintained in this country will forever stand as the crowning glory of the work of the men of colonial days.

Two hundred and fifty-seven years have passed since the first written instrument creating a government was signed at Hartford. This, says Fiske, "marked the beginning of American democracy." Within that time, short as it may seem compared to the age of the leading nations of Europe or to those of antiquity, a mighty people have arisen, and, throwing aside the theories of the nations that preceded them, they have established a government upon principles never before recognized as the basis of civil power, confidence in the multitude, in its honesty, its intelligence, its patriotism—confidence, in short, in the dignity of man. Marvelous has been our growth, and grand our achievements; but does continued prosperity await us? I share in no degree the fears of those who see nothing but clouds above our heads, and hear no sounds save those of convulsions beneath our feet. I believe that the republic of America was never so strong in all the elements of life and power as it is to-day. But society both in this country and in the old countries is entering upon a period of intense unrest produced by the spread of education and the demand for a solution of those problems which have been called forth by the material and industrial progress of the present generation. The liberty of speech which our institutions allow, and the fact that our population to-day comprises all grades and conditions of mankind, must make the discussion of these questions with us especially relentless and bitter. As if to put democracy to the most severe test that could be devised, we permit all who will to come, and almost upon their arrival clothe them with the sacred rights of citizenship. The idle, the worthless and the criminal, even he who sees only in social chaos his ideals of human existence, and would supplant the emblem of liberty with the flag of anarchy, is allowed an equal voice with him whose ancestors and kindred sleep in the unmarked graves upon every battlefield of the Republic. From the adoption of the Constitution to 1820, a period of thirty-one years, the total immigration to this country was 250,000 persons. From 1880 to 1890 it exceeded five and one-half millions. During a single year in that decade it reached the startling figure of 789,000. Certainly it could not have been contemplated by those who framed the Constitution that we should ever receive within so short a time such an enormous influx of people who are strangers to our laws and customs and in no way prepared for our social and political life. Every attempt to modify our naturalization laws or to restrict immigration arouses the opposition of the politician and the demagogue and awakens the fears of party leaders; while every extension of the right of suffrage or the removal of a barrier to immigration is applauded as an act done in the name of humanity.

The growth of private fortunes is creating in many of our people an ambition for the social distinctions and privileges which exist under other forms of government, and is exciting in the poorer classes feelings of envy and bitterness, while labor ceaselessly demands before the doors of corporate power its real or fancied rights and rewards.

Perhaps the greatest danger to our system of government and to our liberties lies in the growing indifference to public affairs of a large portion of our well-meaning and educated citizens. The day when the caucus and primary recorded the verdict of the party in the choice of candidates is gone, and I believe gone forever, and they serve now only to record the wishes of the professional politicians.

Other causes of discord and discontent exist, and other dangers which threaten us might be named, had not the discussion of them long ago been rendered familiar to those I address, by the scholars, writers and statesmen of New England. For here, as in no other part of our country, have the teaching and wise counsels of the fathers been cherished and revered, and any departure from them met with reproval. Indeed, I should crave your pardon, my friends and kindred, for having touched at all upon so trite a subject, did not the circumstances under which we are met and the occasion seem irresistibly to force the mind into this channel, to awaken within us a sense of duty as men, and to appeal to our pride and patriotism as citizens.

The rights and privileges for which the Puritan contended are now accorded to a large proportion of mankind, and in no land save ours more freely than in that from whose oppression he fled. The dangers which beset his life are gone, but new perils have come. The work of the Puritan is not done. Time has mellowed and smoothed away the asperity of his religious views, but it has left us his habits of industry and frugality, his high sense of personal honor, his bravery and moral courage, his love of learning, his integrity and economy in public affairs, his respect for law, his devotion to the cause of freedom, his attachment to his country, and his reverence for God ; and not until these principles regulate the conduct of all who inhabit this land will the labors of the Puritan be finished. Until that time shall have come, his brave and dauntless soul must stand guard upon the turrets of our temples of liberty and progress. By the unalterable laws which constituted his rules of life must American manhood be measured ; by his standards of right and wrong must questions of governmental policy be determined. From no other course can come the solution of the problems that confront us and protection from the dangers that menace us.

Men and women in whose veins flows the blood of Thomas Munson, the preservation in history of the deeds and virtues of our ancestor imposes upon us added obligations to society and to our country.

Through the vista of two centuries and a half we may discern his commanding figure standing upon the rugged shores of New England, in the full vigor of his early manhood. For eight and forty years he walks within our view. As though conscious that every step he takes would be subjected to the light of after ages, he turns not once aside from the pathway of duty. His fellow-men appeal to him and he answers ; the church demands his services, and he responds ; the colony calls to him for protection against the savage and its foes, and proudly he stands forth scorning the fear of death. Oh, my kindred, how rich in example, how worthy of emulation was the life of him who sleeps in yonder grave. Not one of those who are here assembled, or of the thousands who have borne his name ; not one of his descendants who on subsequent battle-fields have won renown, or in literature, the arts, or sciences, have achieved distinction, but might turn with pride and salute him, *Sire*. And here to-day, amid the scenes of his life, let us resolve that his noble convictions of right and duty, inspired by the immortal truths of religion and his high standard of integrity and honor, shall be forever preserved by all who bear the name of Munson.

PROGRAMME AT DINNER.

Chairman.

C. LaRue Munson, Esq., - ' - - Williamsport, Pa.

Vice-Chairman.

Mr. Edward G. Munson, - - - - Cohoes, N. Y.

TOASTS.

1. INTRODUCTORY, - - - - - The Chairman.

2. "THE MUNSON RECORD,"
   The Rev. Myron A. Munson, New Haven.

At the call of the Chairman :

3. Mr. Edward G. Munson, - - - - Cohoes, N. Y.

4. Mr. Rowland B. Lacey, - - - - Bridgeport, Ct.

5. Mr. Stephen Munson, - - - - Chicago, Ill.

6. Harlan L. Munson, Esq., - - - - Westfield, N. Y.

7. Chaplain A. M. Griffith, - - - - Sabina, O.

8. C. M. Bushnell, Esq., - - - - Buffalo, N. Y.

☞ In the evening, the company will occupy Harmonic Hall and parlor for social intercourse, musical entertainment by volunteers, etc.

MENU.

Broiled Spring Chicken.　Currant Jelly.　Cold Turkey.　Cranberry Sauce.

Lamb.　Potato Salad.

Cold Tongue.　Cold Ham.　Sliced Tomatoes.　Celery.

Chicken Salad.　Lobster Salad.

Wine Jelly.

Round Jelly Cakes.　Assorted Cakes.

Neapolitan Ice Cream.

Fruit.　　　　　　　　　　　　　　　Mottoes.

Coffee.　Tea.

TOASTS AND AFTER-DINNER SPEECHES.

This department* of the day's observance was opened with an address by the presiding officer, C. LA RUE MUNSON, Esq.

LADIES AND GENTLEMEN, *Cousins and Joint Descendants of an Honored Ancestor:*

I greet you.

The gastronomic portion of our programme being completed, post-prandial oratory is now the order of the day. That you will suffer no disappointment in listening to those who will be called upon to fulfil that duty, I am well assured. Your toast-master, however, feels that the occasion will not be made more happy by that which he may have to say, and fears that you may find yourselves somewhat in the position of Michael Casey, at his wife's funeral. The undertaker approached him at the end of the services, and said, "Mr. Casey, the religious part of these obsequies are now closed and you will take the first carriage with your mother-in-law." To which Casey replied, "I am quite willing to have all the arrangements duly carried out, but the whole pleasure of the occasion is now spiled."

Could any occasion be more pleasant than an assemblage of the descendants of an honored ancestor? Gathered from various parts of our broad land, we meet to honor the name and memory of one who had no small part in forming the government under which we live, and in securing the civil and religious liberty of which the American citizen can so

---

*As the remarks of those who responded to toasts were extemporaneous, and as no notes were taken of them, the editor has requested the speakers to write out responses, comprising what they said, or may have said, or might have said.

well be proud. In making the assertion that our Colonial ancestry had its share in the foundation of our government we do not misstate the facts nor give to those of our forefathers any undue credit. From want of knowledge of our early Colonial history, the American people have been too apt to give all the honor to the heroes of the Revolution. Their respect and reverence is equally due to those who first settled these shores and made possible the later American Union. The successes of the Revolution were won by the training the Colonial soldiers, and their forefathers, had in the early French and Indian wars. Washington's military strategy and skill were acquired in the forests and morasses of the Ohio Valley; Yorktown, Saratoga and Trenton, were won by the brave soldiers of the Pequot and King Philip Wars, and of the early battles of the West and South. The Declaration of Independence was the natural daughter of Magna Charta. The principles of liberty, embedded in the hearts of Thomas Munson and the men of his times, and brought by them from Mother England, blossomed in the souls of their sons into an indissoluble Union. The eternal principles of equal rights to all men, and a desire for a government by the people, for the people and of the people, which led the Puritan across the stormy Atlantic to an almost unknown and barren shore, bore fruit in his grandchildren in a constitution which has stood the test of time and has been pronounced by an eminent writer to be, next to Holy Writ, the most perfect exposition of human rights ever written.

Few of us appreciate the Puritan influence upon American history, American government and America's commercial industrial progress, as well as upon her religious and educational control of the hearts and minds of her citizens. Let it be the proud boast of New England's sons that, go where they will, in all this broad land, in every city, in every town and village, in every community, small or great, and inquiring of its prosperity, of its achievements and of its civil and religious progress, it will be found that all have been fostered, if not largely secured, by those in whose veins flows the blood of the Puritan settlers of the New England Colonies. Such a Puritan was Thomas Munson and such a citizen was our famous ancestor : his blood pulses in our veins, and so far as we are filled with patriotism and a desire to do noble deeds and achieve a place of honor among our fellow citizens, we can attribute a part, at least, of those characteristics to an inheritance from our honored Pilgrim Father.

To enliven the moment, although tending somewhat to the ridiculous, may I tell a little story I lately read in a comic paper, which humorously illustrates a worthy desire to affiliate with Puritan blood? The scene was a darky ball, and the characters a dusky maiden and her escort, tricked out in the finery in which some of that race are so prone to adorn themselves. "Mistah Johnsing," said the maiden, "Is you one of those who can trace their blood back to de Plymouth Rock?" "I can't say, Miss Fairfax, dat I can do that, but I got hol' of some Plymouth 'Rock chickens one moonlight night, and de nex' day I could trace my blood along de road I came over for more than fo' miles."

We have with us one of the descendants of Thomas Munson, whom I would honor as a Munson second only to our great ancestor. For twelve long years his whole time has been devoted to recording the history of the deeds of that ancestor, and to the records of his descendants. How well he has performed that labor his most successful Munson Record well testifies. Admittedly the best genealogical record yet published, and likely to be long without a rival, and never to be surpassed, his work is an honor, not only to himself, but as well, to the whole Munson Family. It was prepared without reward, or hope of reward, but there will be a reward for him more honorable and lasting than gold or silver could buy. When all of us are mingled with the dust; when our very names, except as he has preserved them, have perished; when every Munson now living has been forgotten, his name will remain a shining luminary in the firmament of the family. No marble shaft or stately granite need mark his resting place, for he has erected a monument to his name and fame which neither time can efface nor years destroy. It is with the greatest pleasure that I present to you a Munson of the Munsons; a true descendant of Thomas, an Elisha who is entitled to wear the mantle of an Elijah, our Family historian, the Rev. Myron A. Munson.

For the generous appreciation of THE RECORD, so hand-somely expressed by yourself, Mr. Chairman, by the orator of the day, and by the other speakers at the morning session, I tender my cordial thanks.

A young girl expressed dissatisfaction with a sermon which she had heard. "What was there that you did not like?" one inquired. She replied, "The beginning was good, and so was the ending, but it had too much middle." You may listen cheerfully to the beginning of my speech, and will certainly be pleased at its ending; but you are suspicious, as I also am, of the rest of it; for is not the speaker he who gave such magnitude to the Munson Book, and is not that book the theme prescribed to him? The speaker will be on his guard.

This is Munson Day: "A red-letter day," do you suggest? Not quite that; it would require all rich and splendid colors to letter it properly. A lady whose home is beyond Lake Michigan, wrote us that she expected to arrive, unattended, in the evening, and would be pleased with an escort to her lodging. To aid in identification, she gave some description of herself; one item was that she was five feet two inches in height. When I saw her this morning she was five feet eleven inches! And I believe that we are all several inches taller than usual to-day.

Fourteen years ago there was not a Munson in the land, so far as I am aware, who knew his lineage through more than four or five generations; not one who knew anything of his pioneer ancestor. And the great Family was unknown to itself; each person knew a few relatives, but the Family at large was as unknown to itself as the western hemisphere was unknown before Columbus. It remained to be discovered. And not only was it a *terra incognita*, but there was little interest in questions respecting the membership of the Family. Our relatives had to be educated into a care for this knowledge, had to have a desire for it kindled, and very interesting have been the manifestations of progress continually bubbling into view.

An impression has been repeatedly mentioned that Connecticut is the principal abode of the Munsons. In the earlier generations it was, but how changed is the situation to-day.

We have found 135 localities in Connecticut where our Munsons have dwelt ; but in Ohio we have found 144 such localities, and in New York, 346. The total number of places discovered in which the descendants of Thomas Munson have dwelt is 1,590 ; of these, 1,531 are in the United States. Can you take in the significance of this amazing fact, that our Family has occupied 1,531 strategic points in forty-eight States and territories ? Why should not the Republic go right and be a good place to live in when ten thousand Munsons occupy all the valleys and plains, prairies, hillsides and mountain-tops, inculcating correct views and forming public sentiment in accordance with an enlightened Christian patriotism ? If society were ever to behave itself and be happy, must it not be under the tutelage and guidance of the sons and daughters of Thomas Munson ?

Just at this point it occurs to me that the Munsons have taken a hand in fashioning the exemplary State of Pennsylvania. They have occupied therein as many as seventy-eight stations, and from those stations have radiated illumining and elevating influences towards all points of the compass. Behold, then, a State whose intelligence, social order, prosperity and general happiness are preëminent. Pardon an oversight : Pennsylvania is a republican State,—just the kind of commonwealth which every judicious democrat wishes to live in ! Imagine our eloquent and esteemed chairman, La Rue, consenting to reside under any other *régime!* You couldn't get him out of Pennsylvania with the help of a regiment of cavalry or a cyclone.

I may mention, finally, two considerations which have afforded cheer as I prosecuted my interminable task. One was that the results of my exertion might be expected to amplify the happiness of the Family. What joy of the life that now is may be compared with that which springs from the love of kindred, each for each, and each for all, and all for each ? If the pleasures springing from family affection are multiplied ; if those whose hearts warm with kinship towards us and towards whom our hearts warm, are multiplied by a hundred or a thousand, must not such acquisitions enrich life inexpressibly ? It seems to me that my own gratification with this mortal career, has been doubled by the discovery of my new-found, long-lost relatives.

The other consideration to which I alluded was this : my confidence that a general and intimate acquaintance with the admirable members of the Family whose light is shining from ocean to ocean and from bay to gulf, and—still more impressively—with our admirable forefathers whose light now shines only from history and from heaven,—my confidence, I say, that a general and intimate acquaintance with such would exert a potent influence in ennobling the present and succeeding generations. The quality of our Family is unquestionably superior ; to contribute to the further elevation of its tone is a function which the speaker deems not unworthy. How many and bright ideals does the Family history present ! And how animating are the varied spectacles of excellence and usefulness ! Does not the sight of aspiring and achieving cousins, the sight of aspiring and achieving sires kindle within us new aspirations and excite us to attempt higher achievements ? The laurels of Miltiades : did they deprive Themistocles of sleep ? O, that the laurels of our Munson laureates may be a perpetual incitement to excel one's present self, to tread with zealous step an ascending path. Sweetness of spirit, fidelity to truth, soundness of character, wealth of usefulness,—such are the excellences which light up a human life with a glow that endures though all the constellations of the sky be extinguished.

(3) Below the great falls of the Hudson, at Cohoes, is a manufactory for the production of health and comfort in the form of nether garments ; its founder and proprietor—prominent among the business men of the Empire State—is a loyal member of our Family, and laboriously devoted to the Family enterprises ; I call upon our Secretary and Treasurer, Edward G. Munson.*

---

* Mr. Munson had already said in his Report at the morning session : Nine years have come and gone since our first reunion. Many who were present at that gathering have passed over to their reward. Our lamented president, Luzerne I. Munson, has gone. Mrs. Grace Munson Wheeler, who was with us then and continued to live to the age of nearly one hundred years, has gone to meet her ancestors, and ours, on the other shore. A number of other starred names will occur to each of us. Many also have come into this active, busy world, lengthening the Family roll-call. Probably a majority of those present at our previous meeting are not with us to-day. Many who were not here then are here now.

I think it fitting to make brief reference to the meritorious services of my predecessor in office, Curtiss J. Monson, Sr. His arduous and efficient labors in promoting and sustaining the former reunion were known to few, but they were praiseworthy and deserving of universal appreciation and gratitude.

Mr. Chairman and Cousins :

Seated in the United-Church chapel this morning, my attention was first called to the fact that my name was on the list of members who, "at the call of the chairman," were expected to say something after dinner in this hall. If my post-office address had not been given I might have imagined it referred to some other Munson bearing the same name.

I know we all enjoyed the exercises in the chapel—greetings, worship, music, addresses, oration, and not least, the Secretary and Treasurer's report in regard to our financial condition. By this report you were advised of the Association's doings from Aug. 17, 1887, to Aug. 19, 1896.

Hard work and much valuable time have been given by those upon whom the duty devolved to make this gathering a fitting conclusion to the preparation and publication of *The Munson Record.*

Much money has been contributed to meet the financial needs. Notwithstanding these pleasant remembrances, we, as an association, are in in debt, mostly to our printing-house, about $900. Any aid you can give the Association in paying this debt will be appreciated.

(4) The Vice-Chairman of the morning session, for many years treasurer of the city of Bridgeport, and employed during a much longer period in responsible public positions, is president of the Fairfield County Historical Society and uncommonly fond of inquiring into local and family history. I call upon Rowland B. Lacey, *ætatis* seventy-eight.

Mr. Chairman and Kinsmen, Ladies and Gentlemen :

It gives me great pleasure to meet so goodly a representation of the Munson Family to-day in this second reunion, and under such pleasant auspices. The only thing unpleasant to me is that I am expected to make a speech. Having informed the committee of the uncertainty of my presence and my wish, in case I might be able to attend, to be entirely inconspicuous, I hoped to enjoy the occasion very quietly, and hence am altogether without preparation. However, since I am here and on my feet, I should be false to my feelings and fail in my duty to our indefatigable historian did I not extend to him and to the entire family my hearty congratulations on the completion of his elaborate and noble work, well and appropriately named the "Munson Record." What might have been a bare genealogical skeleton—valuable indeed for locating the parts, he has succeeded in clothing with so much of personality and achievement that each member of the various clans is introduced to the others, and an interested kinship promoted through the whole family. A noble ancestor, and other noble lives and characters are successively brought to view therein—a benediction and an inspiration for high endeavor to present and future sons and daughters.

I had not extended my researches in my Munson line further back than my great-grandfather, Baszel, of Clan Joel, of New Haven and Hamden. I feel under profound obligation to our historian for bringing to light the records of his useful life—so much in the line of his, and our common ancestor, Capt. Thomas Munson. Esquire Baszel was very fortunate in his family alliances. His first wife was Keziah, daughter of Rev. Isaac Stiles and Esther Hooker, dau. of Mr. Samuel Hooker of Farmington, and great-granddaughter of Rev. Thomas Hooker of Hartford. I make no doubt he was all the more the good and useful man he was, for the meet help she rendered him. She was sister of the half blood of Pres. Ezra Stiles of Yale College, between whom and Esq. Munson and wife there existed an intimate friendship—expressed by an interchange of visits. The grand style and equipage of President Stiles on occasion of these visits to Hamden—which were notable events—made a deep impression upon the children of the neighborhood, and were well remembered and described by my grandmother, Mary (Bradley) Munson.

Undoubtedly Esq. Baszel had a treasure in the wife of his youth and the mother of most of his children, though she died comparatively young. His rare appreciation fairly bubbles over in the inscription on her tombstone standing to-day in the north Hamden cemetery, which I happen to have and I am sure will interest the ladies.

" Keziah
the Excellent wife of Mr. Baszel Munson
She was industrious
She looked well to the ways
Of her own household
The heart of her husband
Safely trusted in her
Her children may rise up
And bless the Memory of
a most affectionate parent
She trusted in the righteousness
of Christ for pardon and Eternal life
and died Oct. 15th, 1773
A.E. tat. 38."

(5) A quarter of a century ago, as you remember, the stores were filled with Munson's boots and shoes. The manufacturer of this well-known footwear, then a citizen of Albany, is with us to-day. He is now engaged in the production of a highly-prized typewriter, "The Munson." I call upon Stephen Munson, *ætatis* seventy-eight, for some reminiscences.

Incidents are facts, and facts form the basis of life. Two young men, one a clerk in the largest dry-goods store of Hartford, the other teller of the Farmers & Mechanics' Bank, determined to form a debating club, and for this purpose asked of Mr. Pomeroy, the President of the bank, if we might have the use of the Directors' room one evening of the week, for this purpose. • His reply was : "Yes, provided I may come in and warm my toes during the evening." The club was formed of thirteen,* six on a side, and a presiding officer. Mr. Pomeroy became much interested in us, and soon proposed to obtain for us the use of the Hartford Library, which was owned by eight gentlemen. Mr. A. M. Collins, my employer, being one of them. This consent was obtained, and the next step was to enlarge our club, these gentlemen assisting us to obtain the use of the City Council chamber. The following season a course of lectures was proposed, and liberally patronized at Gilman's Hall. The next step was the forming of the Young Men's Association, and the donation of the Hartford Library to them on the condition that the proprietors and their families should have the free use of the same. Following this movement, Sirs Collins and Pomeroy proposed to Mr. Wadsworth that he give a lot of land for the site, provided the citizens would donate $20,000.00 to build a building, for the purposes of the Connecticut Historical Society, and the Young Men's Association, and a Gallery of Paintings, which form the present Wadsworth Athenæum of Hartford. All these young men proved good and able citizens so far as I know.

(6) On the southeastern border of Lake Erie, in the grape-growing region, is the pleasant town of Westfield. There and thereabout are many Munsons. They are represented in our gathering to-day by an attorney-at-law. Though he may denominate it—in the lingo of the day—as the crime of '96, I call upon Harlan L. Munson.

----

* Six of these boys were from Chester, Mass., viz., Stephen Munson, William Tinker, William Campbell, John Wright, Aaron Beil, and Henry Collins.— *Ed.*

Mr. Chairman, dear Friends and Kindred:

When our toastmaster tells you he is committing the crime of '96 in calling on one of his own profession to make a speech with but a moment's notice, I can assure you he commits a greater crime than he thinks. Having had comparatively little experience in public speaking, I had determined to devote one-half of my time to telling you of my lack of preparation, and now in his introduction he has robbed me of that half.

However, I am very glad to be present at this reunion and to meet and to form the acquaintance of you, my relatives. With but one exception I have seen none of you before. I am the only representative of a branch of the Munson family which emigrated to Chautauqua County, New York, in 1818, to what was then the frontier. I have heard my grandfather tell of the fatigue and privations of the journey from Oneida County there. The trip was made in the winter through a country without roads or very rough ones. At times they had to follow the beach of Lake Erie and once the wagon became fast in the ice and debris and had to be chopped out with an axe.

I have observed one thing of special interest to me. That is the resemblance in features and general personal appearance of those here to-day and my nearer relatives at home. Those in my country are mostly engaged in agricultural pursuits, but they have what I have observed in you,—those qualities of honesty, sobriety and frugality which makes citizens on whom the state can always depend and which are the fundamental principles of this truly great nation.

I take great interest in meeting you face to face and becoming acquainted with those having with me a common ancestor. I remember my disappointment in childhood when I sought information of my ancestors from my grandfather. He could only tell me that his father came from Oneida County and that his father's people came from Connecticut. By our genealogy we now know it was true, but it was not even then enough for me. I wanted to go back farther.

There are a great many of us out in Chautauqua County. For many years local reunions have been held annually. We would be pleased to have you visit us. Probably many of you have attended beautiful literary Chautauqua and have seen its pretty lake and know something of the country in which we live. Why, Chautauquans believe our county to be the center of the world. Storms and calamities of all descriptions occur around us, but, through all, Chautauquans are untouched and unharmed. If you have never been there, come; if you have visited it, come again. And while there take one of the prettiest drives in the world from Chautauqua Lake over the watershed of the St. Lawrence and Mississippi systems to Westfield on Lake Erie, and call on me and your other relatives, and we will assure you a hearty welcome.

(7) We may think of our Chaplain not only as a preacher, but also as teacher, editor, clerk of his township, and mayor of his city. I call upon the Rev. Absalom Monson Griffith.

This reunion is the most interesting and the most enjoyable gathering I have ever attended. I have been permitted to be a member of some great meetings, a guest at some royal banquets; but this meeting far surpasses them all. I appreciate it because of the privilege it affords of greeting so many of my blood relatives; I rejoice to see you all, and to take the friendly hand of so many of my kindred. Although far removed from our ancestral head, we are still one family. "We are one man's sons." We are his descendants of the eighth, ninth and tenth generations. "One generation passeth away, and another generation cometh;" thus the march of time goes on, and the thousands of our kindred, of former generations, are sleeping the ages away. But in the homes which they vacated, songs and rejoicings were heard over the new-born. Thus the generations have gone on, sorrowing and rejoicing. We also shall lie down to rest by the side of those who fell asleep before us.

This reunion should be a great blessing to us. It should remind us of the great reunion with the "general assembly and church of the first-born whose names are written in Heaven."

(8) The orator of the day may not escape the Toastmaster's attentions. People celebrate their forefathers; they seldom mention their foremothers. I announce as the next and final toast, "The Ladies." I call upon Clarence Munson Bushnell.

Mr. Bushnell made an impromptu response.

MEMORANDA.

The Committee of Arrangements designated by the officers of the Munson Association, expended much effort upon the duties assigned them. The finances were zealously and successfully cared for. Desirable places of meeting were secured and made ready, and a handsome dinner was provided and appropriately served. As to "the feast of reason," let the contents of this pamphlet bear witness. The Committee were efficiently assisted on Reunion day by the Secretary of the Association, by C. J. Monson, Sr., and by Edward B. and Harvey S. Munson.

The weather of August 19th was propitious, and about 200 members of the Family, perhaps a few more, participated in the festivities of the day. As soon as our craft was launched, it was auspiciously wafted onward by Professor Munson's beautiful voluntary on the piano. This meeting of 1896 was made illustrious by Mr. Bushnell's oration. The editor can compare it with no oratorical achievement which he has witnessed since George William Curtis pronounced his eulogy on Sumner, in Boston, twenty-two years ago. The social intercourse of the members of the family was animated, cordial and delightful. From the State of New York, a gentleman writes : "I enjoyed the morning and afternoon exceedingly." Another: "I have most agreeable recollections of my trip to New Haven." From Ohio, a gentleman writes : "It was the most enjoyable event of my life." From Wisconsin : "My mother enjoyed the Reunion of last August exceedingly."

One juvenile attendant gives promise of being good for something. She entertained the company in Harmonie-Hall parlor not only with a violin solo, but also with a recitation, both of them creditable and gratifying. This cousin was E. Gerster Liddle, of Salem, N. Y.

At the Banquet, the Chairman read a telegram from S. L. Munson, Chairman of the Executive Committee of the Munson Association, which was dated at Baniff Hotel, North-West Territories:

"Congratulations to Munsons celebrating Second Reunion. Profoundly regret necessary absence."

Epistolary greetings from others were read. One of these was from Mrs. Sophia Elizabeth Roberts, a Munson of remarkable gifts, and achievements not less remarkable, now seventy-eight years of age. She is a descendant of Capt. Stephen' Munson; her brother, Mr. John Munson, died last Christmas, at the age of eighty-two.

We quote: "It is a disappointment not to be with you *in propria persona*. However, this must not prevent me from expressing my appreciation of the masterpiece accomplished by our Rev. friend and *confrère*, Mr. Myron A. Munson . . . a task arduous in itself and surrounded with difficulties and obstacles so boundless as to have seemed almost insurmountable. I am sure all present will join me in sincerest thanks and appreciation of his wonderfully complete, interesting and beautiful work, a great acquisition to the present generation, and still greater to those who come after and to whom it will be a source of everliving interest."

The Report of the Treasurer, E. G. Munson, presented the following facts:

Received from C. J. Monson, Sr., Treas.,	.	.	.	$159.00
" " membership fees,	.	.	.	184.00
" " portraits,	.	.	.	790.00
" " sales of *Record*,	.	.	.	1830.80
" " Guaranty Fund,	.	.	.	1050.00*
" " other sources,	.	.	.	143.50
Paid Tuttle, Morehouse & Taylor,	.	.	.	3430.00
" Association expenditures,	.	.	.	815.67
Owe Tuttle, Morehouse & Taylor,	.	.	.	797.04
" for other indebtedness,	.	.	.	88.37

Of twenty-seven Guarantors, twenty-one have paid fifty dollars each under their engagement. Forty-four Advance Subscribers have not yet claimed their Books.

The financial executive of the Committee of Arrangements for the Second Reunion, George M. Curtis, reports the following receipts: One dollar from Miss Lillian A. Munson and Dr. W. W. Munson; five dollars, George A. Munson of

* Returned in Books, or returnable in Books or cash.

Smyrna, N. Y., Mrs. Cleora F. M. Judd, Mrs. Robert B. Good-
year, Capt. W. V. McMaken of Toledo, and Harvey Munson
Baker; ten dollars, Mrs. F. T. Proctor, Mrs. T. R. Proctor,
William D. Baldwin of Yonkers, George A. Post of New York,
George M. Curtis, George Munson of Brooklyn, Walter D.
Munson, Edgar Munson, and C. La Rue Munson; twenty-five
dollars, Frank E. Hotchkiss of New Haven; by the sale of
Dinner tickets, $126 ;* total, $268.

The following expenditures: Financial circulars, $1.15,
Reunion circulars and postage, $46.68, ribbon for 300 badges,
$10.50, do. officers' do., $0.52, printing do., and dinner tickets,
$2.75, 400 programmes, $4.25, rent of Chapel, $3.00, janitor's
fee, $2.00, Harmonic Hall, $30.00, Dinner, $135.00.

Balance, $32.15, to be applied to printing the Proceedings,
along with the following contributions for the purpose: One
dollar each, Dr. R. B. Goodyear, Rev. Frederick Munson;
$2.00, F. H. B. Munson, George Munson (Bkln.), Stephen
Munson, John K. Judd, and another (name lost); $5.00, Wal-
ter D. Munson; $10.00, Gilbert D. Munson; $25.00, Clarence
M. Bushnell; total, $84.15. (The Proceedings of 1887, 500
copies, cost $150.05, besides $12.30 paid for design and cut for
the cover.)

We are indebted to the N. Y., N. H. & H. R. R. Co. for half-
fare return tickets over all its roads. Sixty-seven certificates
entitling persons to this advantage, were signed by the Secretary.

☞ A paper prepared by Myron A. Munson on *The Traditions concerning the Origin of the American Munsons*, which was
designed for the Reunion, but for which there was no room,
was published in The Journal and Courier on the morning of
the Reunion. Four points are treated: first, whence did the
Family come, and of what nationality was it? second, what was
the number of Munsons who immigrated? third, what was the
period of the first Munson migration? and, fourth, where,
according to the traditions, did the Family first settle?

---

* Provision was made for 160 dinners.

ADDENDA AND CORRIGENDA.

Proceedings of First Reunion.

Page 35, line 22. Note that in 1653, two pieces were mounted at the harbor, and two placed on the Green. The record of June 14, 1654 made mention of "The great gunns . . at the water side and . . those that stand neere y⁴ meeting house." And again in 1662—three "great gunns" "at water side upon sh— carriages"; three "in the Market place upon field carriages."

Page 46, line 12. The Munson who was "of Newhaven north village" was not Thomas², as was supposed when the Address was prepared, but his son, Thomas³.

The Munson Record.

Page ix, lines 23, 24. Change "Featherby" to *Featherly*.

Page x, lines 4, 5. "Meyer" should be *Myer*.

Page xiv. Add that the abbreviations indicating political and ecclesiastic affiliations, signify simply preference, not necessarily active membership.

Page xix, line 38. Note that the Israel Munson portrait was contributed by Mrs. Helen (Munson) Meaker and Mrs. Henrietta (Clark) Batcheller.

Page xxi. The Motto means, *Ready for my country*. "Prest" is Old French.

Page xxv, line 45. For "Oct." read *Aug*.

Page 167. Add in regard to Stephen⁸ the following items from the new volume of Dexter's *Yale Graduates*: " From 1752 to 1755 he served as College Butler, and meantime he studied medicine, and for a few years (probably not over ten) practiced in the northern part of the town, now North Haven. In 1766 he was employed as a tavern-keeper in New Haven; and later (at least from 1767 to 1783) was deputy-sheriff and keeper of the county jail, which then stood on the western side of the New Haven Green."

Page 374, line 17. Omit " iii. Julia⁹, *d.* 1843, *æ.* 46."

Page 419, line 43. Lillian E.⁹ *m.* 18 Oct. 1871 Charles C. Johnson ; res. Westville, Ct.

Page 749, line 40. Erase *ville* from " Thompsonville."

Page 963, line 41. Change "actor" to *editor*.

Page 1087, line 16. " Caui " should be *Cave*.

REGISTER

France.—
>Clifford F. Snyder, Artist, Paris.

Wisconsin.—
>Mrs. Sarah J. Schoonmaker, Philanthropist, Milwaukee.

Illinois.—
>Stephen Munson, Manufacturer, Chicago.
>Mrs. Stephen Munson, Chicago.

Kentucky.—
>Jacob Frederick Munson, Captain U. S. A., Fort Thomas.

Michigan.—
>Rebecca E. Swift, Teacher, Ishpeming.

Ohio.—
>Abraham Monson Griffith, Clergyman, Sabina.
>Mrs. Mary E. Henderson, Toledo.
>Gilbert D. Munson, Judge, Zanesville.

Pennsylvania.—
>C. La Rue Munson, Lawyer, Williamsport.
>Mrs. C. La Rue Munson, Williamsport.
>Mrs. Fisher Gay, Wyoming.
>Myrtle B. Gay, Bookkeeper (in Scranton), Wyoming.

New Jersey.—
>Charles H. Munson, Manufacturing Jeweller, Newark.

New York.—
>Mrs. Samuel L. Munson, Albany.
>Paul B. Munson, Collegian, Albany.
>Frederick Munson, Clergyman, Brooklyn.
>Mrs. Frederick Munson, Brooklyn.
>Miss Lillian A. Munson, Librarian, Brooklyn.
>George Munson, Purchasing Agent, Brooklyn.
>Mrs. George Munson, Brooklyn.
>Walter D. Munson, Shipping, Brooklyn.
>Mrs. Walter D. Munson, Brooklyn.
>Orange Munson, Farmer, Brookton.
>Clarence Munson Bushnell, Lawyer, Buffalo.
>Edward G. Munson, Manufacturer, Cohoes.

Miss Lydia Munson, Elmira.
Mrs. Mary (Munson) Corliss, New York.
Frederick B. Wightman, Lawyer, New York.
Mrs. Abbie H. Wightman, New York.
Mrs. Mary G. Winslow, New York.
Francis A. Winslow, New York.
Mrs. Cynthia (Munson) Wood, New York.
Henry T. Bronson, Banker (in N. Y. C.), Rye.
Mrs. Henry T. Bronson, Rye.
Mrs. William E. Liddle, Salem.
Miss E. Gerster Liddle, Salem.
Mrs. Adalaide (Munson) Ash, Sing Sing.
George A. Munson, Financier, Smyrna.
Edwin F. Smith, Manufacturer, Syracuse.
Mrs. Clara (Munson) Smith, Syracuse.
Harlan L. Munson, Lawyer, Westfield.

Massachusetts.—

Franklin H. B. Munson,* Lawyer, Adams.
John K. Judd, Wholesale Paper, Holyoke.
Mrs. Cleora F. (Munson) Judd, Holyoke.
Miss Cleora Marion Judd, Holyoke.

Connecticut.—

Mrs. Frank W. Munson, Bethel.
Willard L. Munson, Organist, Branford.
William H. Comley, Judge, Bridgeport.
Mrs. Lucy Isabel Comley, Bridgeport.
Rowland B. Lacey, Treasurer, Bridgeport.
Frederick W. Storrs, Superintendent, Bridgeport.
Mrs. Martha (Munson) Storrs, Bridgeport.
Augustus Munson, Canaan Mountain.
Mrs. George A. Steele, Cheshire.
Dickerman Munson Bassett, Manufacturer, Derby.
Mrs. D. M. Bassett, Derby.
Miss Lillie May Bassett, Derby.
Mrs. Sarah (Munson) Camp, Durham.
Ruth A. Hitchcock, East Haven.
Miss Mary Field Munson, Guilford.
M. Louise Hitchcock, Guilford.
Orrin Munson, Fruit-grower, Hamden.
Mrs. Orrin Munson, Hamden.
Miss Nora A. Munson, Hamden.
William I. Munson, Hamden.
Mrs. William I. Munson, Hamden.
Mrs. Julia R. Simpson, Hamden.
Edwin D. Swift, Physician, Hamden.

---

*Munson not by birth, but by his mother's second marriage, to Erastus Munson.

John W. Talmadge, Hamden.

Mrs. J. W. Talmadge, Hamden.

Miss Alice Gilbertine Munson, Trained-nurse, Hartford.

Mrs. Augusta (Munson) Curtis, Meriden.

George Munson Curtis, Treasurer, Meriden.

Mrs. George M. Curtis, Meriden.

Mrs. Hattie (Munson) Frisbie, Meriden.

Joseph O. Munson, Clergyman, Middlebury.

William D. Munson, Farmer, Middlebury.

Mrs. Wm. D. Munson, Middlebury.

George L. Munson, Carpenter, Milford.

Mrs. Geo. L. Munson, Milford.

Miss Rosa B. Munson, Milford.

George W. Munson, Milford.

Mrs. Geo. W. Munson, Milford.

George O. Munson, Blacksmith, North Haven.

Robert B. Goodyear, Physician, North Haven.

Anna L. Goodyear, North Haven.

Arthur D. Munson, Farmer, Southbury.

Miss Mary Monson, Southbury.

Thomas H. Munson, Contractor, Stratford.

Burton H. Munson, Carpenter, Stratford.

Raymond B. Munson, Stratford.

Mrs. Antoinette (Bristol) Bates, Wallingford.

Miss Mena A. Bates, Wallingford.

Mrs. Charles N. Jones, Wallingford.

Mrs. Angeline L. Beach, Waterbury.

Mrs. John Burns, Waterbury.

Mary L. Fowler, Waterbury.

Eliza R. Fowler, Waterbury.

Mrs. Henry Leonard, Waterbury.

Jos. Marshall Munson, Farmer, Watertown.

William J. Munson, Merchant, Watertown.

Mrs. Truman Percy, Watertown.

Mrs. Wallace G. Munson, West Haven.

Miss Lillian M. Munson, West Haven.

Mrs. John F. Peck, Winsted.

David F. Munson, Blacksmith, Woodbridge.

John N. Munson, Farmer, Woodbury.

Mrs. Amelia C. Munson, New Haven.

Miss Harriette E. Munson, New Haven.

Edward B. Munson, Manufacturer, New Haven.

Harvey S. Munson, Manufacturer, New Haven.

Mrs. Harvey S. Munson, New Haven.

Miss Marion Catlin Munson, New Haven.

Benjamin S. Monson, Silver-plater, New Haven.

Mrs. Mary Monson, New Haven.

Mrs. Clifford H. Munson, New Haven.

Miss Hazel Munson, New Haven.

Charles J. Monson, Yardmaster, New Haven,
Mrs. Charles J. Monson, New Haven.
David C. Monson, Foreman, New Haven.
Mrs. David C. Monson, New Haven.
Miss Frances T. Munson, Teacher, New Haven.
Miss Emily C. Munson, New Haven.
Frederick T. Munson, Salesman, New Haven.
Mrs. Fred. T. Munson, New Haven.
Mrs. Hawkins W. Munson, New Haven.
Clarence A. Munson, New Haven.
James D. Munson, Car-painter, New Haven.
Mrs. James D. Munson, New Haven.
Lyman E. Munson, Lawyer, New Haven.
Myron A. Munson, Clergyman, New Haven,
Mrs. Myron A. Munson, New Haven.
Mrs. Stella E. Monson, New Haven.
Miss Edith Dale Monson, New Haven.
Whitney C. Monson, Carpenter, New Haven.
Albert C. Monson, Mechanic, New Haven.
Mrs. Anna Z. Monson, New Haven.
Miss Anna M. Monson, New Haven.
Mrs. Sarah J. Bailey, New Haven.
Mrs. Jane S. Baldwin, New Haven.
Mrs. Martha A. Buckingham, New Haven.
Mrs. Sara (Munson) Candee, New Haven.
Mrs. M. J. Cargill, New Haven.
Mrs. Clayton G. Cooke, New Haven.
Mrs. Ellen E. (Munson) Curnow, New Haven.
Mrs. Mary (Munson) Frisbie, New Haven.
Mrs. Elias M. Gilbert, New Haven.
Mrs. Samuel D. Gilbert, New Haven.
Mrs. Harriett S. Goodsell, New Haven.
Mrs. Mary S. Goodsell, New Haven.
Clarence M. Gourley, Engineer, New Haven.
Mrs. Lillian J. Gourley, Music-teacher, New Haven.
Miss Lottie Belle Gourley, New Haven.
Mrs. Hattie E. Hitchcock, New Haven.
Hattie M. Hitchcock, New Haven.
Frank E. Hotchkiss, Superintendent, New Haven.
Mrs. Lillie (Monson) Johnson, New Haven.
Mrs. Curtis K. Nickels, New Haven.
Nathan W. Oviatt, New Haven.
Mrs. Nathan W. Oviatt, New Haven.
Mrs. George W. Sanford, New Haven.
George F. Tuttle, Genealogist, New Haven.
Mrs. Lillian (Munson) Strong, New Haven.
Miss Florence Strong, New Haven.
Mrs. Frank L. Wallace, New Haven.

THE MUNSON RECORD

A Genealogical and Biographical Account

OF

CAPT. THOMAS MUNSON

(A Pioneer of Hartford and New Haven)

AND HIS DESCENDANTS

BY

MYRON A. MUNSON, M.A.

Two volumes, royal 8vo, pp. 1267.

CRITICAL NOTICES.

The first work on our list is the Munson Record, in two noble volumes, of more than six hundred pages each. The author, Rev. Myron A. Munson, of New Haven, Connecticut, deserves great praise for the admirable manner in which he has performed his work. . . . The book is carefully compiled. Everything illustrating the history of the family or the individual members—portraits, fac-similes of documents and records, charts, maps, gravestones and autographs, have been gathered and preserved here. The book is handsomely printed, and the illustrations are numerous and of a high order of merit. The indexes are full. We would recommend it as a model for works of the kind.

The New-England Historical and Genealogical Register
for April, 1896, p. 242.

Elaborate and praiseworthy work. . . . Much critical acumen is manifest throughout the work, a sample of which has forcibly impressed us in the foot-note on page 625, where an important error which had passed unchallenged for over one hundred and fifty years has been corrected. The illustrations . . are of a high order. Nearly one hundred pages of carefully prepared indexes close the work. The mechanical execution . . does credit to the Tuttle, Morehouse & Taylor press. . . It will have a large sale.

The New-York Genealogical and Biographical Record
for April, 1896, pp. 110, 115.

462 Beacon St., Boston, Feb. 27, 1896.

MY DEAR MUNSON:

I congratulate you on the completion of your work, and on the two large volumes you have produced. The family ought to present you with a gold medal.

Yours very truly, WM. S. APPLETON.

Estimates of Persons for whom the Book was Prepared.

I have had an opportunity to give a pretty careful examination to the Munson Family Record, which arrived a few days ago. I want to express my entire satisfaction with it, and to say that it even exceeds my best anticipations.

Attorney C. LARUE MUNSON,
(*Lecturer to Yale Law School.*)

I send my hearty congratulations to you, on the great success you have achieved. Your long years of labor are certainly rewarded by a glorious result. I am indeed proud to be found between the covers of such volumes. . . . We are all so much pleased with the family portraits.

Mrs. RICHARD HENRY GREENE,
235 Central Park, West, New York.

I should judge that you and your friends might be fully satisfied with your work. I congratulate you most heartily.

Mrs. JOHN K. JUDD, Holyoke, Mass.

Allow me to congratulate you upon the admirable record you have compiled.

Attorney ALBERT J. MYER, BUFFALO, N. Y.
(*Son of the general and meteorologist.*)

One Yellow Leaf from the Munson Tree sends thanks and congratulations to the Rev. Myron A. Munson.

Mrs. FRED. B. WIGHTMAN,
63 East 131st Street, New York.

They are very fine books.

(Mrs.) FRANCES A. BENEDICT,
363 Adelphi Street, Brooklyn.

How keenly we have enjoyed The Munson Record. It is a most interesting work. . . . W.'s picture in the book is capital.

Mrs. WALTER D. MUNSON,
664 Lafayette Avenue, Brooklyn.

Stupendous task . . . successfully accomplished. . . . That the labor has been enormous is apparent upon every page. . . . These volumes are of inestimable value to-day; they will be priceless fifty years hence. The arrangement of the work is so perfect that I believe these volumes will be used by future genealogists as a model for their works.

Attorney CLARENCE MUNSON BUSHNELL,
Buffalo, N. Y. *(amateur genealogist.)*

I am very much pleased with it. I am amazed at the extent of the work and the completeness of it.

GEORGE E. MUNSON, Seneca Falls, N. Y.

We are so delighted.

LILLIAN M. BASSETT, Derby, Conn.

I have seen no family history that compares with it for detail and exhaustiveness of research.

MYRTLE B. GAY, Scranton, Penn.

A monument to your patience and indefatigable research. We are all to be congratulated at the outcome.

Attorney FRED. W. MUNSON, Chicago.

Since the arrival of the Munson Book we have discarded all other literature, and are giving our days and nights to the study of ancestors. We are wholly pleased with it—matter, form, and everything. Apparently there are a good many small potatoes in the Munson hill, but they seem to be sound, and you have succeeded in giving an individuality to each particular tuber, which is remarkable. What shall we say to the historian to whom we are indebted for recovering all this buried treasure of family history? . . . Thomas and Myron A. shall stand side by side as the names we delight to honor; and our gratitude to the faithful Historian shall not be less than our respect for the Founder.

MARY (CAMPBELL) MUNSON, Manchester, Vt.

Am very much pleased with it. Am very thankful.

Miss LYDIA MUNSON, Elmira, N. Y.

What a tremendous job it must have been, and how successful is the result. I congratulate you.

HORACE H. MUNSON, Wilmington, N. C.

I am very much pleased with them.

HORACE H. LOVELAND, M.D., Michigamme, Mich.

I congratulate you upon the successful issue of a great work. It is the best genealogy I have ever seen. I derive great pleasure from turning its pages.

GEORGE MUNSON CURTIS,
(Treas. Meriden Britannia Co.—and amateur antiquary.)

I am delighted with it. O how much time and labor you have given to the work!

Rev. ABSALOM MONSON GRIFFITH, Sabina, Ohio.

I received my uncut volumes on Monday, and my wife says that I keep my ancestors up rather late nights.

JARED HOWES MUNSON, Brooklyn, N. Y.

Yours was a Herculean task, and you have right nobly performed it.

Col. GILBERT D. MUNSON, Zanesville, Ohio,
(Judge of the Common Pleas Court.)

My congratulations are late but hearty. The work was duly received, and has been the delight of my leisure hours ever since. I expected a fine thing. It exceeds my expectation. I think you have been wonderfully successful in the selection of material. As I turn the leaves at random, there is scarcely a page on which I do not find some matter of special interest.

LOVELAND MUNSON,
(Judge of the Supreme Court of Vermont.)

Viva Voce Expressions.

I enjoyed that Book very much,—I enjoyed it very much.

FRANK E. HOTCHKISS,
(A Director of New Haven Colony Historical Society.)

I have seen your book. It is a splendid thing,—It is a splendid thing. It will be an authority for ages to come.

Rev. GEORGE S. DICKERMAN,
(Now editing the Dickerman genealogy.)

WORTH NOTING.

The Munson Record presents 9,258 descendants of Thomas Munson; 4,671 were born with the Munson name, and 4,587 with other surnames—of which there are 657. Mention is made of 1,590 places in which these persons lived, and of 4,176 individuals who became their wives and husbands. One of the six indexes names Outsiders—1,173 of them with 696 surnames.

Many who are not Munsons are liable to find value in the geographical and historical information presented, in the plan of Wallingford settlement, in the plans of the Soldiers' Field at Hartford, and the Ferry Path at New Haven, in the autographs of pioneers of New Haven and Wallingford, in fac-similes of Revolutionary documents, etc.

The present price of the work at our printing-house is Ten Dollars; on (or before) July 15, 1896, it will be raised to Twelve Dollars. Checks should be payable to the order of the Treasurer of the Munson Association, Edward G. Munson, Cohoes, N. Y. (or to Myron A. Munson, New Haven, Conn.)

June 1, 1896.

ADDITIONAL WORDS OF APPRECIATION.

Please accept my congratulations on the excellence of your work and on its admirable publication. . . . Two admirable volumes.—WARREN UPHAM, Secretary of the Minnesota Historical Society.

I have recently examined a great many genealogical works in the State Library at Albany, but have never seen one so complete as this in all the details, and yet so easy of reference.—MARGARET P. (MUNSON) EVANS, Herkimer, N. Y.

Nothing pertaining to any branch of the family or to any individual of the household appears to have escaped your persistent research. . . . The more I examine . . . the greater is my wonder.—REV. FREDERICK MUNSON, 2 Verona Place, Brooklyn.

I am reading the Family *Record* in course with increasing pleasure.—*Ibid.*

Every page is interesting.—ALBERT MUNSON, Burlington, Vt.

The *Record* is a wonderful work, and invaluable to any member of the Family.—HERBERT E. MUNSON, Sanford, Florida.

Your reward must consist in the appreciation of the many who peruse its pages.—CLARA (MUNSON) SMITH, Syracuse, N. Y.

The two grand volumes of *The Munson Record* have given myself and family great pleasure.—F. H. ALDERMAN, Sharon, Pa.

I was intensely interested in your work, and can but wonder how you could accomplish it so thoroughly.—THEODORE L. FRARY, Burlington, Vt.

I am already very proud of *The Munson Record*.—NETTIE L. (MUNSON) WARNER, Wellington, O.

I would not part with my copy . . . for ten times the cost.—HENRY G. STORY, 21 Herkimer St., Brooklyn.

There is only one word in the English language which describes the work, and it is inadequate,—*stupendous*.—DR. EDWIN D. SWIFT, Hamden, Conn.

They far surpass my anticipations. They are a marvel in historic research. —HARVEY MUNSON BAKER, Oneonta, N. Y.

For several days the splendid volumes have been lying at my left hand. . . . I confess both astonishment and admiration in view of your painstaking patience, your extreme care for exactness in details, and your self-sacrificing labors. . . . All this amazes me. It calls for a devotion of which very few men are capable.—THE REV. DR. JAMES W. STRONG, President of Carleton College (Minn.).

www.ingramcontent.com/pod-product-compliance
Lightning Source LLC
Chambersburg PA
CBHW022042080426
42733CB00007B/942